W9-BMQ-677

Twelfth Night

Robert
grade 3

by Lois Burdett and Christine Coburn

FIREFLY BOOKS

A FIREFLY BOOK

Published by Firefly Books Ltd.

Copyright © 1994 Lois Burdett & Christine Coburn

Fifth printing, 2005

First published in April, 1994 by Black Moss Press with the assistance of the Canada Council, the Ontario Arts Council and the Department of Communications.

All rights reserved. No part of this publication may be reproduced, stored in a retrieval system or transmitted in any form or by any means, electronic, mechanical, photocopying, recording or otherwise, without the prior written permission of the Publisher.

Library of Congress Cataloguing-in-Publication Data is available.

Canadian Cataloguing in Publication Data

Burdett, Lois, 1952–
    Twelfth night for kids

(Shakespeare can be fun)
ISBN 0-88753-233-0

1. Children's plays, Canadian (English).* 2. Children's poetry, Canadian (English).* 3. Readers' theatre.
4. Shakespeare, William, 1564-1616 – Adaptations.
I. Coburn, Christine, 1956-   . II. Shakespeare, William, 1564-1616. Twelfth night. III. Title. IV. Series.

PR2878.T97B87 1999   jC812'.54   C99-932043-2

Published in Canada by
Firefly Books Ltd.
66 Leek Crescent
Richmond Hill, Ontario
L4B 1H1

Published in the United States by
Firefly Books (U.S.) Inc.
P.O. Box 1338, Ellicott Station
Buffalo, New York 14205

Printed and bound in Canada
by Friesens, Altona, Manitoba

Canadä

The Publisher acknowledges the financial support of the Government of Canada through the Book Publishing Industry Development Program for our publishing activities.

Matt Charbonneau, 8

Front cover: Eliza Johnson, 9
Title page: Robert Stroh, 8
Back cover: Kimberly Brown, 8; Jeff Brown, 7

Other books in the series:
A Child's Portrait of Shakespeare
Macbeth for Kids
A Midsummer Night's Dream for Kids
Romeo and Juliet for Kids
The Tempest for Kids
Much Ado About Nothing for Kids
Hamlet for Kids

Foreword

During my time as Artistic Director at the Stratford Festival, I have witnessed the work of Lois Burdett, an inspired and inspiring teacher; plainly founded on love—love of teaching and love of children: idealistic and, at the same time, thoroughly practical.

I first met Lois Burdett in 1986. Her Grade 2—yes, Grade 2—class performed for me their version of a Shakespearean play, rewritten in rhyming couplets. The narrative was spoken in unison by the whole class; Lois conducted: it was an unforgettable and moving experience. The children were totally absorbed in what they were doing: their eyes, their voices, their postures glowed with the kind of joy which arises from group-participation in a creative act. Since that occasion, I have followed Lois's work enthusiastically.

Lois's mission, needless to say, is not vocational: she is not in the business of equipping her class as a kind of theatrical nursery—fostering fledgeling professionals: her vision is far more creative than that. This book articulates that vision and the methods she devised to achieve it.

Lois understands the true meaning of the word *education*—a drawing-forth as opposed to a putting-in by way of imposing knowledge and ideas. She believes that young children (because they *are* young) have wonderful, untapped resources of imagination which, all too often, are allowed to atrophy until it is too late to bring them out and into effective use. Yet without imagination, our lives are crucially diminished.

Lois recognizes that children, properly guided, will take to Shakespeare's characters and stories like ducks to water; in the process they find their inner voices, they collaborate, they improvise, they communicate: they roll back the frontiers of their lives and of each other's.

A Festival governor once told me that the only reason he agreed to add to a busy working life by joining the Stratford Board was because his 11-year-old son (who had been in Lois's class) told him it was his duty! "Out of the mouths of babes..."

Lois's gospel now has numerous evangelists; I am certainly one, and I am honoured to have been asked to contribute a foreword to a book which will, I hope, introduce the work of this remarkable woman to a wider public.

—David William
   Artistic Director, Stratford Festival, 1990-1993

THE CHARACTERS

VIOLA	a young woman
SEBASTIAN	Viola's twin brother
CAPTAIN	of wrecked ship
ORSINO	Duke of Illyria
OLIVIA	a countess
MARIA	Olivia's maid
SIR TOBY BELCH	Olivia's uncle
SIR ANDREW AGUECHEEK	Toby's friend
MALVOLIO	Olivia's servant
FESTE	a jester
ANTONIO	a sea captain
FABIAN	a servant

Kate Bean, 7

I have a story from a long time ago;
I'll tell it to you now blow by blow.
There are quite a few people so you'll have to keep track,
But we'll sort them out, you just sit back...

Dulcie Vousden, 7

It's a beautiful day as our story begins,
But look who comes here. Could they be twins?
Yes indeed, they look the same,
She is Viola; Sebastian is his name.
Like peas in a pod, they were always together,
But this would soon change, due to the weather.
They left in a ship with a captain and crew.
The sun was shining. The sky was blue.
Indeed, they were having so much fun,
They didn't see the clouds cover the sun.

6

Suddenly the air turned bitterly cold;
The wind picked up a thousandfold.
It tore at the mast. It slashed at the sail.
Sebastian cried, "Viola, it's a gale!"
The Captain bellowed, "All hands on deck,
I fear there's to be a terrible wreck!"
The sailors on board were filled with despair,
"She's coming apart! Quick say a prayer!
Have mercy on us. The end is near.
We don't want to die!" they shouted in fear.
The battered ship was tossed to and fro;
They were all trapped with nowhere to go.
With a sickening crack the boat hit a rock.
Viola screamed and collapsed in shock.
"My life is over," she said with a moan.
"Don't leave me now. Don't leave me alone."

Dan Barker, 9

Sebastian desperately reached for her hand,
"I love you sister. Do you understand?"
With that, a wave smothered the ship,
And the ravaged boat began to tip.
As they were tossed and pitched into the sea,
Viola cried, "Captain, hang on to me!"
He held her tight for what seemed like days.
The lightning flashed. The sky was ablaze.
Somehow or other they made it to shore.
Then the storm stopped. It rained no more.
Viola searched for Sebastian in vain,
"Will I never see my brother again?
Did you see him, Captain? Answer me fast!"
"I did, my lady, clinging to the mast."
Viola smiled, "At least there is hope;
That gives me the strength I need to cope."

VIOLA

Erin Bick, 8

Nicky Walch,

But Captain, pray tell, where are we?"
"My lady, Illyria is where we be."
"And who," she asked, "is in charge of this place?"
"The Grand Duke Orsino. They call him Your Grace."
Viola said, "I've heard of this man;
Tell me more of him, if you can."
The Captain replied, "If he has his way,
A countess will be his fiancée.
I speak of Olivia, but she's in such pain.
I fear she'll never date again."
Viola was shocked, "I wonder why?
Is this girl nuts? She doesn't want this guy?"
"It's been said she'll see no man at all,
Since her father and brother died last fall."

Brittany Shaw, 7

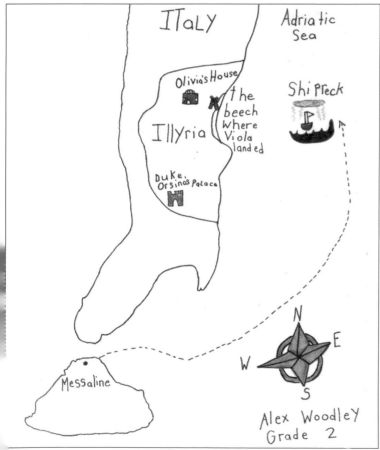

Alex Woodley, 7

9

"Well enough of this chat," Viola said,
"I need a place to lay my head.
I must have a job to earn a wage,
Perhaps Orsino needs a page."
"Well, my lady, you can't be a dame.
How about Cesario for your name?"
"Yes indeed, and I'll need a sword;
I think I can fool this lord."
The Captain replied, "A mute I'll be,
I won't snitch. You can count on me!"

Captain

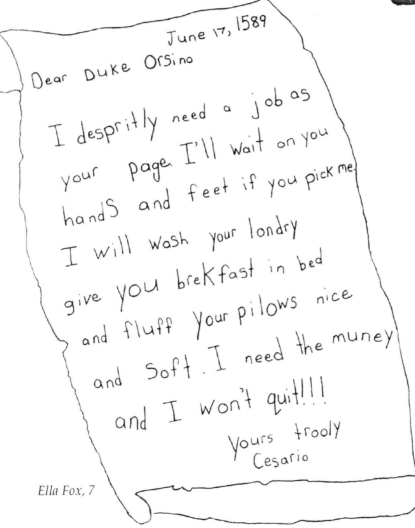

June 17, 1589

Dear Duke Orsino

I despritly need a job as
your page. I'll wait on you
hands and feet if you pick me.
I will wash your londry
give you brekfast in bed
and fluff your pilows nice
and soft. I need the muney
and I won't quit!!!
Yours trooly
Cesario

Ella Fox, 7

10

That very same day at Orsino's place,
The Grand Duke sat with a very long face.
"Come musicians, play me a song,
But not something loud. It would be wrong.
If music be the food of love,
Play like the angels from above."
They'd just begun when he cried, "No more!
'Tis not so sweet now as it was before."
Just then a servant appeared in the hall,
"I've been to Olivia's to pay her a call.
I have some news but it's not so hot;
Your plans for her are completely shot.
She'll wear a veil to cover her tears
And see no one for seven years."
Orsino was touched by her devotion,
"I want her so!" he cried with emotion.
"If love for her brother runs that deep,
When she feels my love, her heart will leap."
Orsino pranced across the hall,
"Maybe there's hope for me after all."

Music: Lisa Coburn, 8
Verse: Ian Ferguson, 8; Patrick Henry, 8

Dear: Olivia PRIVET Just Do not touch!
Love girl!
I love those little dimples
on your smooth face. I love you
right down to your toe nails. Your
lips are red as a cherry. You're the
gal for me. I gaze at you. I dream
about you all night long. You must
marry me. You're the key for
my life. YES or no? If it's not
yes I'll be shreded wheat. You
and me were ment for each other
Come to me. I'll die with
out you. ANSER!
Your love bug Orsino   Jeremy

Jeremy Thiel, 8

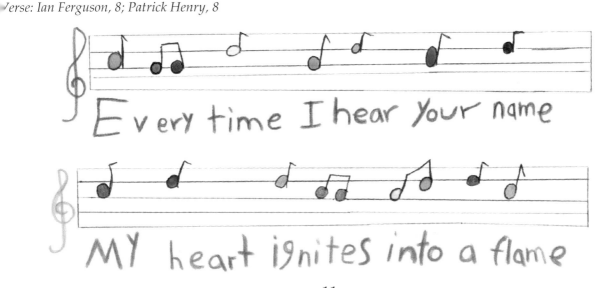

Every time I hear your name

MY heart ignites into a flame

While things looked up for Orsino His Grace,
It was a different story at Olivia's place.
Olivia moped in her room feeling sad,
But Maria, her maid, was steaming mad.
She scolded Sir Toby, Olivia's kin;
He seemed to be leading a life of sin.
"You're home too late to get your sleep.
Olivia hates the hours you keep."
Sir Toby Belch just shrugged her off,
"What's it to you if I drink and quaff?"
Maria continued, "And that's not all;
I've heard of your friend who comes to call."
"Ah, this man of whom you speak,
He is Sir Andrew Aguecheek.
He's filled with charm and skill and wit."
Maria snorted, "He is a twit!"

Maria

Kimberly Brown, 8

To Sir Toby Belch

Sir Toby please try to stop drinking and eating and staying out so much. Sir Toby every time I come to dust I find your muddy shoos on the carpit. I'm sik and tired of shampooing the rug every time you have those wild parties. From now on you clean the place!!
from Maria

Alicia Buck, 7

Dear Maria,
Excuse me but keep you nose out of my Bisness listen to me. We WILL be partying. So get used to it!
from Sir Toby

Jillian Brown,

Sir Toby replied, "He's not that bad,
If he wed my niece, I'd be quite glad.
He loves to drink to Olivia's health;
What's more, he is a man of great wealth.
But hush, Maria. Here he comes."
They greeted each other, the best of chums.
They talked such nonsense and utter rot,
That Maria left, fed up with the lot.
Sir Andrew's smile turned into a frown,
"I think I'd better leave this town.
Your niece won't have me," he woefully said.
"I'm sure it's the Duke she's going to wed."
Sir Toby yelled, "No, that's not true.
What girl would turn down a catch like you?'
Sir Andrew agreed, "You are quite right.
For one more month I'll hang in tight."

Sir Andrew Aguecheek

Adam Robinson, 7

Sir
Toby
Belch

Ashley Kropf, 9

Meanwhile, back on Orsino's land,
Cesario, the page, was lending a hand.
Viola's disguise had worked like a charm;
She had no trouble twisting his arm.
Orsino had fallen for Viola's white lie;
He really believed she was a guy.
But this little game was soon out of control,
For Orsino had touched her very soul.
"I wish he knew I am not what I seem,
I think he is a perfect dream."
When Orsino called her to come right away,
Viola rushed in without delay.

Cesario

Ashley Kropf, 9

Duke Orsino
Give up the girl! She
won't have you. You
are never going to
win her hart. Anyway
choclits make your
teeth rot and presents
are not made of Love!!
            Alex Woodley

Alex Woodley, 7

14

"There is a job you can do for me,
Olivia, the countess, I want you to see.
Stand at her door. Do not be denied.
Tell her I want her by my side.
Explain that I love her. I'll always be true.
My speech will sound better coming from you."
Viola wanted to say, "Get a life,
If you really want someone, I'll be your wife."
But she didn't say what was in her heart,
Instead she smiled, "I'll do my part."
So Viola set off to do the job,
Although inside, she wanted to sob.
She pulled down her hat as before,
Then marched right up and knocked on the door.

Lindsay Mavity, 10   Viola

Orsino you should give up on Olivia. Find yourself a new wife. You are giving her a masive headake!

Jeff Brown

Jeff Brown, 7

I think Olivia should give Orsino another chance. If Olivia's lonely, marrying him can't be that bad. I would marry him because he has lots of money. Plus, he would give me great mother's day gifts!!!

Katie Brown GR2

Katie Brown, 7

I think Olivia is being very rood to Duke Orsino. I say :
MARRY THE GuY!

Courtney Chadwick

Courtney Chadwick, 7

A servant, Malvolio, peeked through the crack,
"Olivia is busy. You'll have to go back."
Viola insisted, "I must see her,
I'll stand right here 'til you concur."
"Hang on," Malvolio said with a sneer,
"I'll go and see. You wait here."
Malvolio strutted, his nose in the air,
"My lady, there's a strange man out there."
Olivia said, "Who could it be?
Oh send him in so I can see."
She pulled her veil down over her face,
Then she and Maria each took their place.
Viola came in and looked at the two,
"Tell me Olivia, which one is you?"
"Never mind that!" Olivia did say,
"Where are you from? What part do you play?"
"I've come from Orsino to plead his case,
But I'll go no further 'til I see your face."

Dulcie Vousden, 7

Malvolio

Amy Robinson, 9

Olivia relented and lifted her veil;
Her face was exquisite in every detail.
Viola began to read her speech;
She dropped to her knees and did beseech.
"My master loves you with sighs of fire.
You are his only heart's desire."
Viola kept reading line after line.
Olivia gagged, "He will never be mine.
His sickly words make my stomach churn,
Leave right now! But please return."
Viola left with a look of dismay,
"Orsino won't be happy today."
But Olivia's face was filled with delight,
For she had fallen in love at first sight.

Dear Olivia I Love thee so will you please please marry me! If you do we will be the happiest couple in the whole world. I'm on my hands and knees for you. You can have children and your favorite food for dinner every night!

Pretty please!

Love Orsino

Jennifer Stewart, 7

Dear Dear Olivia I'll do anything for you. Will you marry me my darling? I will climb the highest mountain and jump off... but I'll take a parishoot.

Orsino Olivia

I love thee So Orsino

Alison D.

Alison Dickens, 8

But how could she win Cesario, the lad?
She took from her finger a ring that she had.
She called Malvolio,"Run after that man.
Return this ring to him if you can.
Tell him Orsino's not my kind of guy.
If the lad comes tomorrow, I'll tell him why."
Malvolio moved at a frantic pace.
He caught Viola and snarled in her face.
"Give this trinket back to your boss;
It's making Olivia very cross."
Malvolio turned and went on his way.
Viola just stood there, "What a weird day!
I didn't leave a ring behind.
Could it be I've lost my mind?
This band of gold, what does it mean?"
Then she remembered the looks she had seen.
"I think the countess has fallen for me;
Olivia knows not that I am a she.
And I love Orsino, who really loves her.
What have I done for this trick to occur?"

Ali Kara, 7

VIOLA'S DIARY

Dear Diary 1589 July 2
I have trooley fallen in love with a boy. His name is Orsino. He smells like roses in the valey. His eyes are like shining fairy dust. I have been so foolish. I drest up as a boy to get a job and now I cannot show my love. I wish my brother were here to help me. I cannot be without Orsino. Oh Diary what can I do?

Lauren Gr. 2

Lauren Vancea, 7

Dear Diary:
I am madley in love with Orsino. I hope with all my hart and sole that he will marry me. I love him more then life it self!   Viola

Back at Olivia's later that night,
Sir Toby's room was filled with light.
He was with Sir Andrew and a clown, Feste,
"It's party time! Hip hip hooray!"
It was going great 'til Maria stomped in,
"Olivia's fed up with all this din."
They partied on. They didn't care.
Sounds of laughter filled the air.
The party was a real blast,
Then Malvolio entered, his face aghast.
"I've come from Olivia, so out of my way!
Just listen to what she has to say.

Let's Party!

Sir Andrew Aguecheek

Toby Belch

Adam Robinson, 7

Feste

19

Olivia's had enough of this noise.
Now put away your silly toys."
Malvolio left them in a stupor.
Sir Toby yelled, "Party pooper!"
Maria agreed, "The guy's a jerk!
I have a plan for him that will work.
We'll make a love note written in code.
When he figures it out he will explode!
It will be from Olivia, and it will say
That she loves Malvolio more each day.
We'll meet tomorrow to do the trick.
She'll think he is a lunatic.
I can't wait," Maria said,
"But now it's late. I'm going to bed."

That night some silly caracters were throwing a party. They dansed like Wild. But mean nasty Malvolio smashed into the room. Smoke came out of his eyes. His cheeks were as red as the sun. His teeth shivered and his hair stood on end. He scowled at them all. PARTIES ARE DESKUSTING AND TARUBL. GO TO BED

Nicky Walch, 8

Nicky Walch, 8

Sir Toby Belch

Malvolio

20

In the morning, at the Duke's estate,
Orsino was in a very sad state.
"Oh Cesario, life is not fair,
When you want someone and they don't care."
Viola confessed she loved someone too,
"My Duke, this person is much like you."
Viola told him, "If I weren't a boy,
Your love would fill me with utter joy.
But Olivia won't have you. She's made that clear."
That was not what Orsino wanted to hear.
He ordered Viola to take her a jewel,
"Tell her my heart she'll always rule.
She'll change her mind; I have no doubt."
So off to Olivia's Viola set out.

Dear OrSino
You are the pitS! Your giftS are a waSte. Don't take one Step cloSer to my houSe or it'S curtinS for you. JuSt leve me alone!

Signed The Angry
Olivia

MariJke
Grade two

Marijke Altenburg, 7

Duke Orsino

Amy Robinson, 9

That day Malvolio rose quite late,
But his raging anger did not abate.
He didn't know that out on the walk,
Sir Toby and friends were having a talk.
A servant, Fabian, joined in on the fun.
He was mad at Malvolio for things he had done.
Maria was saying, "He's such an old goat,
I know Malvolio will fall for this note.
If we leave it here, I have no doubt,
He'll pick it up, the silly old trout!"
Sir Toby said, "Quick, behind those trees."
So they ran and waited on bended knees.
Malvolio wandered along the path;
His sullen face was filled with wrath.
Just then he spied Maria's letter,
"Should I open it? I guess I'd better."

Matt Charbonneau, 8

He picked up the letter and read it through,
"It's a love note for someone. I wonder who?
It's Olivia's writing; that much is clear,
But why does M.O.A.I. appear?
Wait! All those letters are in my name.
Olivia loves me! You can't blame the dame!
She loves my yellow stockings and garters of black,
If this is love I'll never look back!
But what is this? A little P.S.,
She says I must smile. I'll do my best!"
When he left, Sir Toby laughed with glee,
"Maria, you devil, please marry me!"

Valentine: Lisa Coburn, 8
Words: Ian Ferguson,8; Patrick Henry, 8

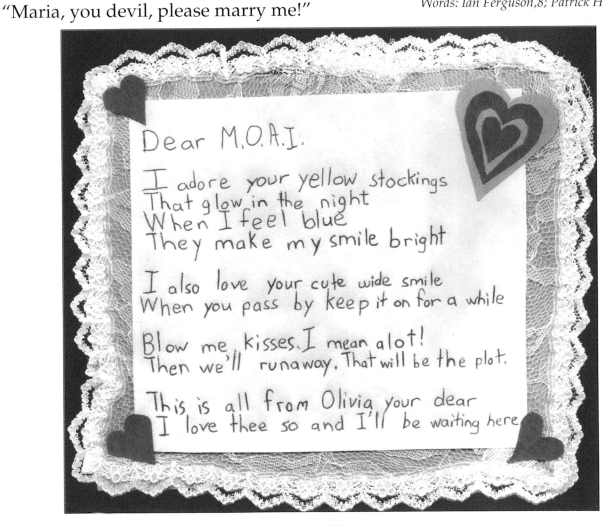

Dear M.O.A.I.

I adore your yellow stockings
That glow in the night
When I feel blue
They make my smile bright

I also love your cute wide smile
When you pass by keep it on for a while

Blow me kisses. I mean a lot!
Then we'll runaway. That will be the plot.

This is all from Olivia your dear
I love thee so and I'll be waiting here

When Viola showed up, not long after,
She'd missed the trick and all the laughter.
She stopped with Sir Toby and Andrew to talk,
Then Olivia and Maria strolled down the walk.
Sir Andrew listened with growing pain
As Viola flattered the countess again.
Olivia told everyone to leave right away,
Except for Viola to Sir Andrew's dismay.
Olivia begged, "Cesario be mine.
It is for you my heart does pine."
Viola retorted, "Give it a rest.
You're acting like a woman obsessed.
Believe me, Olivia, you're way off track.
I'm leaving now and I'm not coming back."
As she walked away she raised her brow,
"If only Sebastian could see me now."

Dulcie Vousden, 7

Olivia   *Jennifer Stew.*

24

But what had happened to Viola's brother?
Had he survived somehow or other?
Yes indeed, he'd made it to land;
A seaman, Antonio, gave him a hand.
Poor Sebastian was filled with dread;
He thought Viola was surely dead.
He thanked Antonio and said good bye,
"Don't stay with me. I'm an unlucky guy."
He headed for Orsino's court.
Antonio followed to lend support.
As they got closer to the duke's place,
Antonio dreaded showing his face.
"I can't go with you," Antonio said.
"There are people here who want my head.
They say years ago I committed a crime.
The Duke is eager for me to do time.
But here is some money, my good friend;
It doesn't matter how much you spend."
As each man parted to go his way,
They decided to meet later that day.

Jeremiah Courtney, 8

Christopher Luckhardt, 8

Sebastian

25

They didn't know that in this town,
Viola had caused many to frown.
In fact, Sir Andrew was ticked at her.
It was time to leave, of that he was sure.
He whined to Sir Toby, "Can't you see?
Olivia thinks more of Cesario than me."
Sir Toby decided to have some fun,
"Don't you see what Olivia's done?
She wants to awaken the lover in you.
She only pretends Cesario to woo.
You should have made him look the fool.
Why don't you challenge the lad to a duel?
Send him a letter with the time and place.
I'll deliver it myself, face to face."
Sir Andrew replied, "What a marvellous caper!"
Then he rushed off to put pen to paper.
Sir Toby rolled on the floor with mirth,
"This is the funniest thing on earth.
The duel will surely be a sight,
With a gentle page and a cowardly knight!"

Sir Andrew Aguecheek

Luc Forsyth, 9

Adam Robinson, 7

Then Maria burst in laughing with glee,
"Malvolio's bonkers! Wait till you see."
When Olivia called Maria to come,
She'd laughed so hard she was almost numb.
Maria wiped the smile from her face,
Then marched right in and took her place.
Just then Malvolio entered in style;
He had on his face a ridiculous smile.
His silly smirk made Olivia cross,
But Malvolio continued to grin at his boss.
"I smile for you, my chickadee,
But I tell you these garters are killing me."
Olivia gasped, "What's wrong with your head?"
"I do this for you," Malvolio said.
"My yellow stockings and garters you love,
That's why I wear them, my turtle dove."
Olivia shrieked, "This man is sick.
Get Sir Toby to help him quick!"

Julie Wilhelm, 8

Malvolio

27

Sir Toby came in as Olivia rushed out;
She'd heard Cesario was somewhere about.
Maria said, "Toby, he's acting insane,"
Malvolio sniffed and spoke with disdain,
"Go hang yourselves," he said with a sneer,
"I'll get you for this. I'm outa' here."
Maria and Toby plotted some more,
"Why don't we put him behind a locked door?"
In a dark room he'll have to stay.
We'll have a blast while he's away.
Just then Sir Andrew walked in on the pair,
Waving his mighty sword in the air.
"Cesario the page is in for a shock.
This challenge will make his scrawny knees knock."
As Sir Andrew read it, word after word,
Sir Toby thought, "This is absurd.
His foolish threat is much too mild;
I'll change it into something wild."
But he didn't say any of this,
And Sir Andrew left in ignorant bliss.

Ian Ferguson, 8

Dear: CeSario
I am getting blud thrsdy
mad. It will be sord to sord
and I will win. I am the Strongest
Knight in the whole of Illyria.
          Sir Andrew Aguecheek
CARL Leushuis

Carl Leushuis, 7

Matt Charbonneau, 8

Sir Andrew Aguecheek
c/o The Countess Olivia

stamp

TO CeSario
DuKe Orsino's Palace
Illyria

A short time later Viola came by.
Sir Toby thundered, "Prepare to die!
I have a friend who is furious at you;
With his sword he'll run you through!"
Viola began to quiver and shake,
"This friend of yours has made a mistake.
I've wronged no man," Viola said.
"I don't want to lose my head."
Sir Toby's story continued to grow,
"The world's best warrior is your foe.
I'll go and tell him you're ready to fight.
A guard is watching so stay in sight."
Sir Toby found Andrew not far away;
He did not speak of Viola's dismay.
Instead, he pretended Viola was brave,
"You should see him rant and rave.
He has the strength of twenty men.
He can't wait to fight again."
Sir Andrew's eyes grew wide with fear,
As Sir Toby grinned from ear to ear.
"I've changed my mind!" poor Andrew cried.
"It's too late for that," Sir Toby lied.

Jeff Brown, 7

To: Cesario
You are making me very jellis,
so, I'm going to challenge you
to "A duel." You'll need extra
muscles to fight with me!
Bewear to "DIE!" You're
probly as scared as a birdy!

Signed: Your worst enemy,

Sir Andrew Aguecheek

Katie Brown, 7

Challenge To... Cesario
Meet me in the woods at
ten o'clock. Don't be a cowerd.
It's going to be sword clashing
madnes!

Sir Toby Belch

Andrea Heyen, 10

29

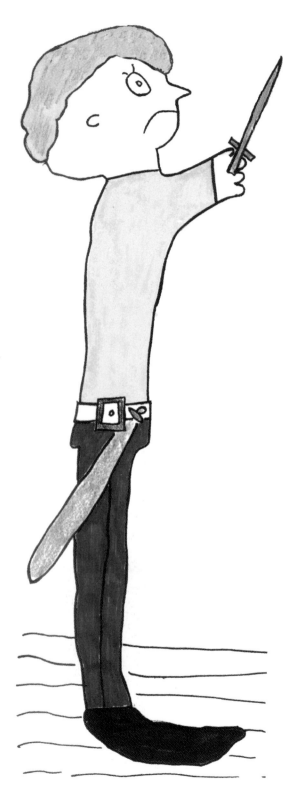

He dragged Sir Andrew back to the place
Where Viola stood with a terrified face.
The two were shoved together to fight;
It really was a comical sight!
Just then Antonio did appear.
He saw Viola shaking with fear.
It was Sebastian, or so he thought.
He stopped the duel right on the spot.
Antonio bellowed, "Don't touch my friend!
This young man I will defend.
While I'm here, he'll come to no grief."
Viola breathed a sigh of relief.
"Who is this guy who saved my skin?"
Before she could ask some guards charged in.
Orsino's troops were everywhere;
They'd heard Antonio the outlaw was there.
"Stop!" they shouted. "You're under arrest!"
Antonio gave up with little protest.
He said to Viola, "I'm in a bad way.
I'll need my money without delay."
"You gave me no cash," Viola said,
"But without your help, I'd surely be dead.
So even though I don't have a lot,
You can have half of all I've got."

Antonio was stunned, "This can't be true,
After all that I have done for you!
Sebastian, I saved you from the sea,
And now you turn your back on me."
With that, Antonio was taken to jail.
Viola felt weak. Her face was pale.
"He called me Sebastian," Viola said.
"Could it be my brother's not dead?"
Viola left in a kind of trance.
Sir Toby gave Andrew a withering glance.
"Can you believe that ungrateful cad?
He turned his back on the friend he had."
Sir Andrew agreed, "And he's not that tough.
Next time we meet I'll be quite rough."
When Sebastian wandered into sight,
Sir Andrew was ready to pick a fight.
He thought it was Cesario the page,
"I'll get you now," he quivered with rage.
Sebastian wasn't worried at all.
He ripped off his shirt and began to brawl.
He fought Sir Andrew, his fists clenched tight.
Sir Toby jumped in to stop the fight.
Sebastian turned on him with his sword,
"One more move and you'll be gored."

Nicky Walch, 8

31

As Sir Toby drew his trusty blade,
Olivia entered in a tirade.
"Sir Toby Belch! Stop right now!
Your rude manner befits a sow!
Leave at once. Get out of my sight."
She turned to Sebastian. Her eyes were alight,
"Cesario my love, I feel such remorse.
My uncle's behaviour is way off course.
Come into my house and stay awhile."
Sebastian agreed with a puzzled smile,
"Is this a dream or have I gone mad?
What happened to the name I had?"
But he thought Olivia could do no wrong,
So like a puppy he followed along.

Jenny Geoghegan, 8

In another part of Olivia's estate,
Malvolio seethed with vengeful hate.
He was locked away in a cold dark cell.
His nose turned up at the musty smell.
He didn't know that out in the hall,
His three tormentors had come to call.
Maria and Sir Toby convinced the clown
That he should wear a preacher's gown.
They wanted to make Malvolio think
He'd gone completely over the brink.
"Malvolio," they called, "you are possessed.
It is quite clear your brain needs rest."
Malvolio cried, "I'm not insane!
I have good reason to complain."
Malvolio pleaded for paper and light,
"A letter to Olivia will make things right."

Dear Olivia
Don't you care? I admire you more than you can imajin. Please bail me out my Sweet Love. I am as thin as a bone. I did not do anything to deserve this. If I don't have you I think I will die.
Your Hunny Bunch
Malvolio

Marijke
7 years old

Marijke Altenburg, 7

Dear Olivia,
With all my heart, please let me free.
I only did what you told me to do.
And now, I'm in jail, cold and thin.
I'm flabbergasted! I'm crushed!
I'm "ANGRY"!
Signed: Your Down in the Dumps,
Malvolio.
Katie Brown
Grade 2

Katie Brown, 7

Mike W.
7 yrs old

Mike Williams, 7

Meanwhile, Olivia was with a real priest;
She was ecstatic to say the least.
"Finally I've won Cesario's heart.
Now we're together, we'll never part."
She turned to Sebastian and went down on one knee,
"I love you Cesario. Will you marry me?"
"Okay!" said Sebastian. His eyes were aglow,
"To you, sweet lady, I would never say no."
"All right!" Olivia said with a cheer,
"I've longed for you. Now I've got you, my dear!"
They both agreed to always be true,
Then went to the church to say, "I do."
While Olivia had found wedded bliss,
Others in our tale could not say this.
Life for them was one big mess;
They hadn't found true happiness.
But Fate would playfully intervene,
And bring them together for one last scene.

Amberly Henry,

Olivia

Robyn Lafontaine, 7

34

The Duke arrived at Olivia's gate.
He and Viola were told to wait.
As they lingered, there came down the street,
Antonio and officers of the Duke's fleet.
Orsino remembered Antonio's face,
"You're the enemy I tried to erase."
Antonio proudly said, "That's true,
But I've also helped the fellow with you.
In fact, I rescued him from the sea,
And ever since he's been with me."
"You lie," said Orsino. "You are a louse.
For the past three months he's been at my house."
Before he could say another thing,
Olivia entered, flaunting her ring.
She smiled at Viola, "My husband, you're great."
Viola gasped, "I'm not your mate!"
Olivia was shocked, "This cannot be.
Here is the priest to vouch for me."

Cesario

Nika Mistruzzi, 10

Brittany Shaw, 7

35

Orsino turned on Viola with rage,
"How could you do this, you back-stabbing page?"
Olivia, Antonio and the Grand Duke,
All glared at Viola with looks of rebuke.
As if that weren't enough for her,
Sir Andrew stormed in, his blood astir.
He pointed to Viola, "You broke my head.
Look at my bloody wound," he said.
Then Toby ran in, "Get a doctor now!
Cesario has clobbered me on my brow."
Viola just stood there, "This can't be true.
What is wrong with all of you?"
Then who should walk in, larger than life,
But Sebastian, full of concern for his wife,
"I'm sorry I hurt your uncle back there."
Olivia just stood, with a frozen stare.
She didn't know what was taking place;
There were two people with her favourite face.
Sebastian didn't see. He just carried on.
He said to Antonio, "I thought you were gone."
Then he came to Viola. His heart skipped a beat,
"Who's this fellow I'm about to meet?"
He wondered aloud, "Am I going mad?
You look like the brother I never had."

Sir Andrew

Carolyn Parr, 9

Dulcie Vousden, 7

Viola thought she'd seen a ghost,
"My brother was lost just off the coast."
It took a while but they finally clued in
That they were each other's long lost twin.
The Duke was watching this scene unfold;
He thought Viola was solid gold.
"You are a girl!" he said in surprise.
"Yes I am," she said with twinkling eyes.
"Let's tie the knot!" Orsino cried.
Viola gushed, "I'll be your bride."
Just then Feste rushed in with a note,
It was the letter that Malvolio wrote.
Feste began to read the plea,
'My dear Olivia, set me free.
You locked me up for worshipping you;
I thought by your love note you wanted me to.
You've done me wrong. Now let me go.
From the Madly Used Malvolio."

Wedding Rules
DO'S
1. Do polish your shoos
2. Do shampoo your hair
3. Do wear your tukseedo
4. Do pray for sunshine
DON'TS
1. Don't be nervis
2. Don't be sick
3. Don't miss saying "I DO"
4. Don't forget to read this list!

BY Ella

Ella Fox, 7

37

Olivia listened with growing doubt,
"What's all this talk of a love note about?
I need to hear what he has to say."
She sent for Malvolio without delay.
Her servant, Fabian, led him back;
Malvolio was pale and thin as a rack.
"My Lady Olivia, do not deny,
You wrote me this love note. I ask you why?
You told me to wear these garters of black,
Then locked me up like a maniac."
"I didn't write that," Olivia denied,
"It's in Maria's hand," she cried.
Fabian was quick to take the blame,
"I helped to bring this man to shame.
And Sir Toby Belch had the time of his life,
Along with Maria, who is now his wife."
Malvolio was not in the mood to forgive,
"I'll hate you all as long as I live!"
But although he remained a bitter soul,
Not so Feste, who kept up his role.
His lot in life was to clown and jest,
And that is what Feste did best.
He began to sing one final song,
In a voice that grew ever strong.

Malvolio

Sarah Micks, 9

When that I was and a little tiny boy,
With hey, ho, the wind and the rain,
A foolish thing was but a toy,
For the rain it raineth every day.

A great while ago the world begun,
With hey, ho, the wind and the rain,
But that's all one, our play is done,
And we'll strive to please you every day.

Feste

Marissa Izma, 9

To Parents and Educators:

Each year, thousands of people pass through theatre doors and into the world of Shakespeare. Traditionally, few children have been encouraged to enter this magical world. This initial exposure has often been delayed until the child's high school years. It is our belief that Shakespeare can be meaningful and fun for children of all ages. We hope this book will assist you in exploring the antics of Twelfth Night. Here are a few suggestions you might find helpful as you share this book with your children.

- *Use the poem as a Readers' Theatre. The dialogue can be acted out by different children, with the narrative done in chorus.*

- *Let the children act out the play in their own words using puppets or costumes.*

- *Have each child explore a character's viewpoint through writing diaries, letters, challenges and other items such as those you have seen in this book.*

- *Encourage the children to use their artistic creativity in activities such as designing costumes, drawing maps and building the stage in miniature.*

- *Above all, have fun!*

Lois Burdett's Grade 2 students perform *Twelfth Night* on the Stratford Festival stage. From the left: Nicky Walch, 8, as Sebastian; Stuart Wilson, 7, as the Captain; Jennifer Stewart, 7, as Viola. Photo by Scott Wishart; courtesy of The Beacon Herald, Stratford. Above, Brad Jesson, 7, as Pyramus for *A Midsummer Night's Dream* staged in Lois's Grade 2 classroom.